Starting Games Skills

ANDREW COOPER

Stanley Thornes (Publishers) Ltd

First published in 1995 by:
Stanley Thornes (Publishers) Ltd
Ellenborough House
Wellington Street
CHELTENHAM GL50 1YD

A catalogue record for this book is available from the British Library.

ISBN 07487 2093 6

Typeset by Tech-Set, Gateshead, Tyne & Wear.
Printed and bound in Great Britain.

Acknowledgements

This book has been completed with the help and advice of Celia Harvey and Jean Walton, 'experts' in encouragement!

My thanks to 'model' Helen Wittrick for her help with the illustrations.

Contents

Foreword

This book offers help with games skills lessons taken by class teachers of Reception and Key Stage 1 children. It is concerned with the teaching of travelling skills, with and without equipment, and sending and receiving skills and structuring simple games. These 'games' involve interaction between partners and groups in co-operative and competitive contexts, and the development of understanding of rules.

The Schemes of Work cover the Programme of Study of the Physical Education National Curriculum in Reception and Key Stage 1 in a progressive series of lessons.

Each year group section is preceded by a breakdown of the activities covered and the intended learning outcomes for travelling, sending and receiving. This overview is intended to assist longer term planning of the Scheme of Work and to show progression within each skill area.

The material is structured into lessons which build on the general principles of skill acquisition for this age group. Each lesson can be the basis for further sessions. Advice is given on the bridge between Key Stages 1 and 2.

This book will provide a basis for planning and delivering games for primary generalist teachers and give help and guidance to Physical Education Curriculum Leaders on a Scheme of Work for Key Stage 1 Games.

Starting Games Skills and *The Development of Games and Athletics Skills* provide a complete Scheme of Work for Key Stages 1 and 2.

A Key Stage 1 principles

(i) The focus is on the individual learner. Tasks are matched and modified so that all children achieve success at their own level and have opportunities to improve. This implies that tasks are based on the developmental stage they have reached, taking account of individual physical attributes.

(ii) The content of lessons should be based on a broad repertoire of skills. It is useful to categorise them into:
- travelling: footwork skills (running, dodging, jumping, etc.)
- travelling with (e.g. dribbling, carrying) a piece of equipment
- sending away (e.g. passing, throwing, striking)
- receiving (e.g. moving to stop, catch or trap).

(iii) As well as providing this broad range, each category should contain variety (e.g. striking with foot, hand and implement, using different sizes of ball, different size and shape of bats and sticks, different distances, targets, heights, speeds and angles). This allows children to broaden and deepen their skill learning so that the acquisition of new skills can easily be accommodated into their growing experience.

(iv) This principle of variety has an implication for lesson structure: each lesson should contain some travelling, sending and receiving skills, and involve children in situations where they play alongside each other with a partner, using these skills in games which are teacher-structured. Children will be able to devise their own games based on the skills learned. This process helps to develop understanding of the need for and use of rule structures. It is therefore important to set tasks so that each child can be successful at his/her own level, focus on effort rather than ability and make extensive use of co-operation.

B The learning of skills

There are three types of skill to acquire, all of which require the child to process information just as they would in a Reading, Writing, Science or Mathematics context:
- 'closed' skills – skills performed in predictable, unchanging environments (e.g. rolling a ball towards a stationary target);
- 'open' skills – which take place in constantly changing environments (e.g. the situations that occur in small-sided team ball games);

1

- 'serial' skills – skills in between closed and open (e.g. dribbling a ball around obstacles, or receiving a ball through a target from a partner).

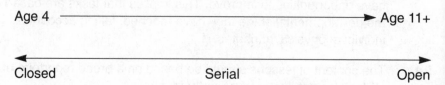

Age 4 ⟶ Age 11+

Closed　　　　　　　　　　Serial　　　　　　　　　　Open

Most infant game activities tend towards the closed end of the continuum. It is obvious that a young learner cannot process, memorise and make decisions about masses of complicated information, so keep the teaching points and demonstrations brief.

A different teaching strategy will apply to the more open skill of receiving (stopping, trapping and catching) than to the more closed skill of sending a ball to a stationary target. Receiving requires the child to process information about the sender's action, distance, direction, ball speed and trajectory (flight path), predict where and when the ball will arrive, move the body and hands, foot or implement into the appropriate place and then use the appropriate technique to stop the ball. Sending does not require these complicated anticipatory decisions. Therefore, when teaching an open skill, alert the child to the relevant points (it is useless to know how to hold your hands if you cannot predict where the ball will arrive!) and when teaching a closed skill teach the best way to perform an action.

C The bridge between Key Stage 1 and Key Stage 2

The development of skills in games-like contexts means that children in the 6–8 age range can be introduced to activities which begin to bridge the gap between learning skills and applying skills (understanding and decisions) in the context of:
- net-type game situations
- fielding-type game situations
- invading territory-type game situations.

Using skills in a developing context implies:
- that the child can begin to apply skills learned to game-like situations (e.g. skills learned in Maths to attempt investigations, or Writing skills to explain a Science activity)

- that the child can make anticipatory decisions in a game-like situation based on some understanding of the form or structure of the game being played.

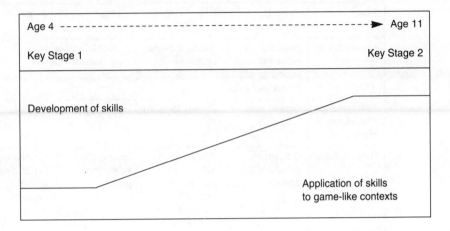

You will find 'Pre' invasion, net and fielding activities after the Key Stage 1 lessons (see page 81).

D   Summary of principles of primary games development

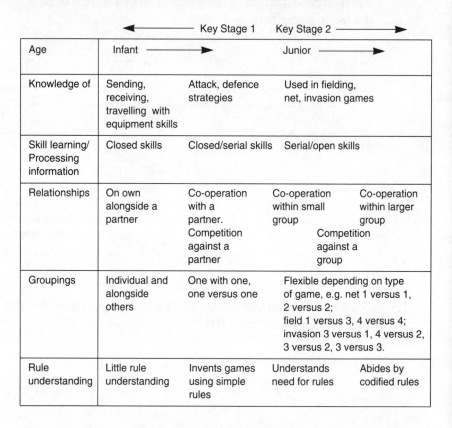

	Key Stage 1		Key Stage 2	
Age	Infant ——→		Junior ——→	
Knowledge of	Sending, receiving, travelling with equipment skills	Attack, defence strategies	Used in fielding, net, invasion games	
Skill learning/ Processing information	Closed skills	Closed/serial skills	Serial/open skills	
Relationships	On own alongside a partner	Co-operation with a partner. Competition against a partner	Co-operation within small group. Competition against a group	Co-operation within larger group
Groupings	Individual and alongside others	One with one, one versus one	Flexible depending on type of game, e.g. net 1 versus 1, 2 versus 2; field 1 versus 3, 4 versus 4; invasion 3 versus 1, 4 versus 2, 3 versus 2, 3 versus 3.	
Rule understanding	Little rule understanding	Invents games using simple rules	Understands need for rules	Abides by codified rules

The development of a school policy statement and Schemes of Work are based on these principles of development and planning.

A   Progression

The Physical Education processes Planning, Performing, Evaluating, are well defined in the Physical Education National Curriculum Non-Statutory Guidance (Section D, 1.0). The progression principles of difficulty, variety and quality are incorporated into all the lesson material.

In this book the progressions used for each year group are reviewed at the start of each year section, so that class teachers can relate them to the Programme of Study for Key Stage 1 games when planning units of work. Teachers should use their own judgement at the beginning of each year to decide when to start on the Lessons with their class. Teachers of Reception classes may use pre-Lesson activities which introduce children to using the hall and playground space, colour groups and equipment organisation.

The progressions in teaching games skills to Reception, Year 1 and Year 2 children are small and incremental. Practice and repetition is desirable to develop such skills. In all three sections in this book the lessons are progressive and should be taught in order. Each Lesson can form the basis of several short sessions. Use your judgement to decide when to progress your class. The developmental material is revisited and extended in each year section.

Children of the same age are at different stages of development, e.g. some can and some cannot hop or skip, and therefore tasks are designed so that they can be made easier or harder to suit individuals. Advice on differentiation is given in individual lesson sections. The principle is: set the task and then modify the task to allow individuals to progress/succeed. For example, for the task 'Roll a ball with two hands to hit the cone' progression could be as follows:

Body part progression   – roll with one hand
Equipment progression   – use a smaller ball
Spatial progression   – move further away
Size of target progression – make target smaller.

In the same way this task can be made easier by using a larger, slower ball, moving nearer and making the target larger.

Children can be asked to make the task easier or harder so that they become involved in the process of evaluation. By using this principle (or by choosing material from another age group) you can accommodate mixed-age classes.

In each section there are two lessons where the children make decisions about the games they will play. This is a device to involve them in structuring the game, thus introducing simple rules and conventions of fairness. They can compete against their own best attempt, but most activities are based on partners co-operating to keep a rally going, increasing participation and skill development. Lessons include individual activities and move on to playing alongside another person, before playing in co-operation with a partner. There are some small group activities at the end of the Year 2 material.

Travelling progressions
At the earliest stages pieces of equipment (cones, quoits, hoops, etc.) are placed in the space so that children can be guided to move on curving pathways. Travelling with a piece of equipment is the essence of games skills, so carrying in hands is followed by foot- and bat-controlled dribbling. Footwork skills such as safe jumping and landing and stopping are introduced in Reception and revisited and improved in Years 1 and 2. Footwork activities are intended to be vigorous and give teachers the opportunity to help the children to recognise how exercise affects their bodies.

Sending progressions
Rolling with the hands is followed by sending, underarm before overarm, with a bounce, through the air for accuracy and finally throwing for distance. The emphasis when kicking with the feet and hitting with a bat is on accuracy. Because sending is a mainly closed skill the teaching points are about aiming, stance and grip, and evaluating what happened.

Receiving progressions
Receiving skills are the most difficult to acquire because children need to make increasingly open, anticipatory decisions.

Receiving skill progressions are carefully structured so that the decisions children have to make are generally in line with their development. The sequence followed is:

1 receiving a rolling ball
2 receiving a ball bounced several times
3 receiving a ball bounced once
4 receiving through the air/high trajectory.

To begin teaching receiving to children aged 4–5 by asking them to toss a beanbag into the air and catch it, is to build failure into the task for the majority of children. Receiving from rolling is *predictable* because it does not require complicated decisions about trajectory (flight path), which small children find very difficult to predict. Progression is then to rolling to the side, which makes the receiver watch the hands of the sender closely in order to move to where the ball will arrive, as well as getting their hands to stop/catch it at the right time. Stopping the ball in this way should be praised as a catch because the correct anticipatory decision has been made.

Interaction

The Key Stage 1 Programme of Study Games states that pupils should be taught:

'(a) Simple competitive games, including how to play them as individuals and, when ready, in pairs and in small groups.'

The General requirements (2) require teachers to 'develop positive attitudes ... (a) to observe the conventions of fair play, honest competition and good sporting behaviour ...'

Pupils should be taught: '(b) how to cope with success and limitations in performance and (c) to try hard to consolidate their performance.'

In Key Stage 1 children will be working towards these statements. All children should be encouraged to try hard to achieve their best performance.

Competition, that is test of skill, against one's own performance (e.g. rolling a ball to hit a target – succeed – now make it harder by using a smaller ball/target/moving further away) is one of the basic techniques by which teachers motivate children and enhance their individual performance.

In order to practise and consolidate performance or try new skills, children will work on their own and with others. Sharing equipment with someone else in the context of a partner activity needs to be taught. The purpose of sharing (co-operating) is to practise to consolidate quality performance. The type of competition which has a negative influence on performance can be avoided by emphasising individual skilled performance.

All the partner activities and simple games in this book include aspects of co-operation and competition – they are tests of the children's own skill and understanding, and tests against a partner.

The small group activities require a group to co-operate in order to compete against an individual, e.g. possession ball (3 versus 1) or striking/fielding games (1 versus 3).

Participation
The guiding principle is that all children should be involved and active all of the time.

Relays are not used in this book to teach or practise games skills. A relay activity is defined as one where children are in teams, e.g. one child runs, the rest wait in turn or pass a ball through the legs.

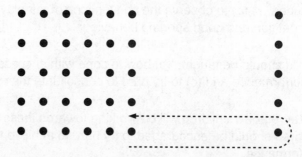

This type of organisation allows only five children to participate while 25 spectate! Relays are often overcompetitive and lead to breakdown of skill and loss of self-esteem for the unsuccessful. They do not help team-work. They are not *Physical Education*. The material in this book is designed for maximum participation – the opportunity for all children to gain pleasure and enjoyment through playing 'games'.

B Lesson structure

(i) Introductory activity/warm up

This is often a vigorous footwork activity or travelling individually with a piece of equipment, using and learning about moving skilfully with others in a restricted space.

The introduction establishes your control. Listening carefully to instructions sets the tone of later activities which demand co-operation and problem-solving.

(ii) Introduction or development of individual skill or skills with a partner

Set tasks which can be modified for individuals. Adjust the variety and difficulty by asking the children to make the task easier or more challenging depending on their degree of success. Ask them: How did you do it? What did you change? (e.g. distance, speed, the type of ball or bat, the size or shape of the target). Use problem-solving in this way to engage children actively in their own learning, decision-making and evaluation. Don't be afraid to:

- teach a specific technique; e.g. how to hold the hands to catch, if it is appropriate
- limit the task; e.g. 'Everyone try dribbling the ball with the inside of your feet.'

Children want to be able to perform a task well. Repeat a practice, emphasise different aspects of the task, set different targets – challenge them!

(iii) Introduction or development of activities alongside or with a partner: the beginning of playing a 'game'

- Teacher-structured games where specific skills are expected to be used.
- Children can be asked to develop their own rule structures. This teaches them about the purpose of and need for rules. Give the children some guidance (equipment, purpose, challenge): e.g., 'Make up a passing game using two cones, two ropes and a ball. Make your game harder when you can play it well.'

9

Check the safety of their setting out. A variety of solutions will emerge based on the principles you have taught. Intervene to reinforce and deepen learning. Learners should know the purpose of the task and what they are trying to achieve.

(iv) **Concluding activity**
A warm-down activity – return to an individual or partner practice or a choice of one aspect of an individual skill. Travelling activities are most useful.

Apparatus should be put away carefully and safely.

C **Observation**
Observation is the key to successful teaching and learning. Guidance on what to look for or teaching points is given after every skill task and game. This information implies that the teacher knows the criteria involved and is capable of observing these planned criteria or teaching points.

In teaching Physical Education the observer has to 'video' the action (there is no written evidence!), decide what the child did well and how to help that individual (or group). This is not an easy task but it is essential to master this teaching strategy in order to assess pupil progress and ensure that each child achieves success.

D **Task-setting and guidance**
Set tasks with clear expectations. Observe the children's performance against your teaching point criteria. Give specific advice on skill technique; e.g. how to hold the bat or how to process/attend to the appropriate information (such as watching the sender's hand as he/she releases the ball) or strategy.

Demonstration (by pupil or teacher) is a powerful visual aid in conveying a teaching point. Bring pupils round in a semi-circle so all can hear and see. Draw their attention to the important points of the action before the demonstration, and then let them practise the part or whole skill or strategy.

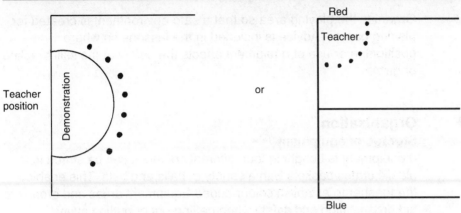

Demonstration can also be used to foster the observation and evaluation skills of pupils. Give positive feedback which tells the child what they have done correctly, then add praise and a further challenge. Always use the child's name: 'Gurdip, your grip is correct, the arm started straight, and your stance is sideways. That was well done. Can you speed up your arm action next time so that the ball travels further?'

Watch the next attempt and give praise. Giving positive feedback about teaching points and performance criteria lets the child know the correct technique and helps improve performance. Giving value-loaded feedback: 'That's OK, Chris. That was great, Andrew,' confuses because no criteria is used. Giving negative feedback: 'Your throwing stance is hopeless, Ravinder,' destroys confidence.

E   Safety
When helping individuals or teaching groups, keep on the outside of the area so that everyone is in view. The corners give the widest angle.

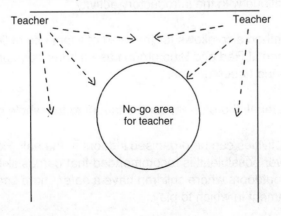

Organise the playing area so that a safe environment is created for playing games. Advice is included in the lessons on where positioning or use of equipment affects the safety of the skill practice or game.

F   Organisation
Storage of equipment
If equipment is bought in four different colours it can be stored in plastic crates/baskets with a variety of balls and bats. This enables the teacher to establish colour-coded Equipment areas and groups to aid organisation and safety when getting out or putting away equipment.

Yellow equipment	Red equipment
Green equipment	Blue equipment

This sort of organisation also makes it easy to introduce the next activity. The most common method used in this book is to teach the next activity to two colour groups (e.g. Red and Blue) while the other two continue with the introductory activity.

This method also allows for the most efficient use of limited equipment if Red and Blue groups use different equipment from Yellow and Green groups.

The material, if preferred, can be taught to the whole class.

Most activities can be organised indoors in the hall. However, whenever possible, it is recommended that games skills should be taught outdoors where children have a safer, more spacious environment in which to play.

G   Space

Playgrounds can be organised into playing areas by marking grids of
8 m × 8 m or 10 m × 10 m. Blocks of four are useful for developing
games. Grids are extremely useful for structuring groups of children;
they provide a flexible playing area for most activities, and allow the
teacher maximum observation opportunity.

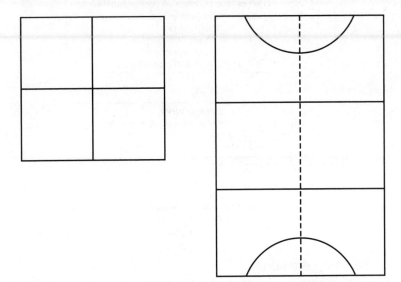

A netball court can be lined down the middle using beanbags/quoits/
cones to provide six grids. Grids can also be marked on grass.

H   The planning process

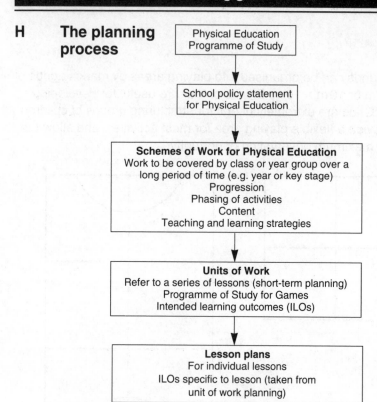

Physical Education
Programme of Study

School policy statement
for Physical Education

Schemes of Work for Physical Education
Work to be covered by class or year group over a
long period of time (e.g. year or key stage)
Progression
Phasing of activities
Content
Teaching and learning strategies

Units of Work
Refer to a series of lessons (short-term planning)
Programme of Study for Games
Intended learning outcomes (ILOs)

Lesson plans
For individual lessons
ILOs specific to lesson (taken from
unit of work planning)

Planning decisions

Each school will have to decide how it is going to cover the Physical Education National Curriculum. Factors concerning the games curriculum might include phasing (the time of year when activities are to be taught), the amount of time devoted to games and how that time is distributed.

From these decisions a whole school policy can be produced which will form the basis of a delivery plan for Key Stage 1 games.

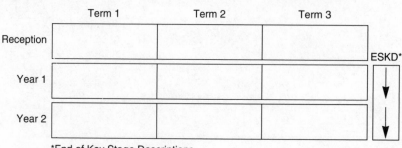

	Term 1	Term 2	Term 3	
Reception				ESKD*
Year 1				
Year 2				

*End of Key Stage Descriptions

Planning decisions for class teachers: Unit of Work

Physical Education Planning: a Unit of Work
1. Programme of Study: Games   Gym   Dance   Athletics*   OAA*   Swimming**
2. Programme of Study: activity-specific information from the National Curriculum
3. Children's previous experience
4. Time available for Unit (No. of lessons per week, lesson time, total time)
5. Resources available: equipment and outdoor/indoor space with diagram of marking
6. Title of Unit: e.g. Gymnastics theme   Age group: R, Y1, Y2, Y3, Y4, Y5, Y6
7. ILOs and statement about progression over the Unit/Term/Year
8. Adaptations needed because of space, safety, equipment, special needs, etc.
9. Teaching methods or organisation comments as result of points 3, 4, 5, 7, 8

*   For Key Stage 2.
** Optional for Key Stage 1.

Lesson structure specific to games, gym, dance, etc.	WEEK 1 number of lessons = ...	WEEK 2 number of lessons = ...	WEEK 3 number of lessons = ...	WEEK 4 number of lessons = ...	WEEK 5 number of lessons = ...	WEEK 6 number of lessons = ...
GAMES: ACTIVITIES TO BE COVERED WEEKLY						
Introduction						
Skills						
'Games'						
Conclusion						

Criteria for Assessment: 'can do' statements relating to whole UNIT (grid or criterion wheel)

Refer to End of Key Stage Descriptions.

H   Equipment
Large-/medium-sized inflatable plastic balls
- round sizes 3 and 4
- sponge/vinyl-coated sizes 3 and 4.

Small balls
- tennis ball cores
- sponge/vinyl-coated 7 cm and 9 cm
- glow/unburstable 7 cm (excellent for throwing/hitting activities)
- airflight/gamester-type 7 cm and 9 cm (excellent for throwing/hitting activities).

Bats
- wooden padder bats with short handles in a variety of shapes
- unihoc sticks.

For marking out, targets, skills practices, etc.
- plastic cones of various sizes
- beanbags
- quoits
- ropes of different lengths
- hoops of various sizes
- wire skittles (useful for making nets)
- garden canes 4–6 ft (useful for making 'nets')
- braids.

It is especially important that learners practise with balls which have a consistent/predictable bounce quality. A variety of different types of ball is essential if tasks are to be differentiated so that all children can take part successfully. Refer also to Appendix 4 Paragraph 4.13.

J   Assessment
Assessment in Physical Education is carried out by observing children in practical, physical activities. The purpose of this ongoing teacher assessment is to:
- identify children's achievements
- diagnose learning difficulties
- measure progress through the National Curriculum Programmes of Study.

Such information about pupils' achievements can:
- tell us if the ILOs are being achieved
- help in planning activities resulting in modified ILOs
- provide feedback to pupils, other teachers and parents
- provide a basis for curriculum evaluation (e.g. content, resources, planning and teaching methods).

The National Curriculum Statutory Assessment Framework consists of End of Key Stage Descriptions for Key Stage 1 (years 1 and 2) and Key Stage 2 (years 3, 4, 5, 6).

Teacher assessments during the key stage will contribute to the report on pupils' achievements at the end of each key stage (i.e. ages 7 and 11). Formative data can contribute to yearly reports.

Planning and assessment
Formative assessments enable the teacher to identify the next stages in a child's learning. The three strands identified in the Physical Education National Curriculum are Planning, Performing and Evaluating.

Children will progress at different rates in relation to each of these categories (e.g. according to levels of physical maturity). To enable children to achieve at their own level, tasks can be set as follows:
- as a common task for all children allowing for differentiated outcomes from different children
- at different levels of difficulty in relation to each task for different children or groups of children.

Pupils should be encouraged to assess their own and other children's achievements.

Collecting evidence of achievements
The main means is by direct observation. A number of performances must be observed before stating that a child is capable of performing a specific skill or task (valid evidence).

The teacher can collect evidence of the children's planning and evaluation. For example, the teacher can ask the children how they are going to perform/have performed a task, or by observing their physical performance in a partner or group game.

Evidence of achievement will be observed in:
- physical skill (Performing)
- selection and organisation of response to a task (Planning)
- describing what they and others are doing (Evaluating).

Level Descriptions in Physical Education
'... describe the types and range of performance which pupils characteristically demonstrate.' (National Curriculum 1995)

Teachers should make a judgement as to which Level Description best fits each pupil's performance.
The Level Description for Key Stage 1 closely follows the Programme of Study and should be used *as a whole* to decide on a pupil's level of attainment.

The primary purpose of Level Descriptions is to guide the teacher towards a summative assessment of the child's performance at the end of the key stage.

Illustrations and diagrams

Throughout this book you will find numerous illustrations and diagrams demonstrating the most significant features teachers should be looking for as children carry out the activities.

Frequently occurring features are illustrated with the following symbols:

- target – cone/skittle/beanbag/quoit

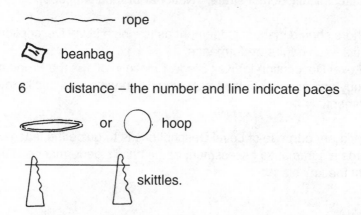

——————————————— rope

beanbag

6   distance – the number and line indicate paces

or   hoop

skittles.

These features will only be labelled if they are used in a way, or for a purpose, different from the one indicated in this key.

General requirements for Physical Education Key Stages 1–4

Physical Education should involve pupils in the continuous processes of Planning, Performing and Evaluating. This applies to all areas of activity. The greatest emphasis should be placed on the actual performance aspect of the subject. The following requirements apply to the teaching of Physical Education across all key stages.

1 **To promote physical activity and healthy lifestyles, pupils should be taught:**
   a to be physically active;
   b to adopt the best possible posture and the appropriate use of the body;
   c to engage in activities that develop cardiovascular health, flexibility, muscular strength and endurance;
   d the increasing need for personal hygiene in relation to vigorous physical activity.

2 **To develop positive attitudes, pupils should be taught:**
   a to observe the conventions of fair play, honest competition and good sporting behaviour as individual participants, team members and spectators;
   b how to cope with success and limitations in performance;
   c to try hard to consolidate their performances;
   d to be mindful of others and the environment.

3 **To ensure safe practice, pupils should be taught:**
   a to respond readily to instructions;
   b to recognise and follow relevant rules, laws, codes, etiquette and safety procedures for different activities or events, in practice and during competition;
   c about the safety risks of wearing inappropriate clothing, footwear and jewellery, and why particular clothing, footwear and protection are worn for different activities;
   d how to lift, carry, place and use equipment safely;
   e to warm up for and recover from exercise.

(The National Curriculum Orders January 1995.)

Key Stage 1 Programme of Study

In each year of the key stage, pupils should be taught three areas of activity: **Games**, **Gymnastic Activities** and **Dance**, using indoor and outdoor environments where appropriate. In addition, schools may choose to teach Swimming in Key Stage 1 using the Programme of Study set out in Key Stage 2.

Throughout the key stage, pupils should be taught:
- about the changes that occur to their bodies as they exercise;
- to recognise the short-term effects of exercise on the body.

Areas of activity

Pupils should be taught:

1 Games

a simple competitive games, including how to play them as individuals and, when ready, in pairs and in small groups;

b to develop and practise a variety of ways of sending (including throwing, striking, rolling and bouncing), receiving and travelling with a ball and other similar games equipment;

c elements of games play that include running, chasing, dodging, avoiding, and awareness of space and other players.

(The National Curriculum Orders January 1995.)

Attainment target: End of Key Stage Descriptions

The following descriptions describe the types and range of performance that the majority of pupils should characteristically demonstrate by the end of the key stage, having been taught the relevant Programme of Study. The descriptions are designed to help teachers judge the extent to which their pupils' attainment relates to this expectation. The expectations match the level of demand in other subjects and are broadly equivalent to Level 2 at Key Stage 1, Level 4 at Key Stage 2 and Levels 5/6 at Key Stage 3. At Key Stage 4, an additional description is provided to help teachers differentiate exceptional performance.

Key Stage 1

Pupils plan and perform simple skills safely, and show control in linking actions together. They improve their performance through practising their skills, working alone and with a partner. They talk about what they and others have done, and are able to make simple judgements. They recognise and describe the changes that happen to their bodies during exercise.

(The National Curriculum Orders January 1995.)

National Curriculum *Non Statutory Guidance* – games
C5 Games: Key Stage 1

4.13 At the beginning of Key Stage 1 pupils should be allowed to play freely. Lessons should be designed to give maximum activity as well as scope for individual exploration and practice. At this key stage lessons usually involve small apparatus such as airflow balls of assorted sizes, beanbags, hoops, quoits, skipping ropes, small-, medium- and large-sized balls and playbats of assorted shapes and sizes and, where appropriate, specially designed equipment for pupils with physical disabilities. The skills learned will help towards successful work with a partner and in small groups and are important for future success in games.

4.14 Units of Work for approximately half a term could be developed to include aspects listed below:
- Footwork: running, hopping, skipping
- Awareness of space and other people: chasing, dodging, avoiding
- Jumping and landing
- Ball skills: sending using hands and feet and incorporating hitting; receiving; travelling with a ball
- Games: opportunity to make up and play games with simple rules and objectives that involve one person and with a partner when ready.

Reception: scheme of work

	Travelling with/without equipment	Intended learning outcomes P of S	Sending skills	Intended learning outcomes P of S	Receiving skills	Intended learning outcomes P of S
L1	Walking around a space. Walking/jogging carrying a beanbag.	Using curving pathways, avoiding other people and obstacles.				
L2	As L1		Sending towards a target using hands, rolling.	Aiming for accuracy, making the task easier or harder. Evaluation of performance. Stance, sending actions	Retrieving a rolling ball.	Using hands.
L3	Walking keeping a ball under control using the feet. Carrying the ball in two hands.	Avoiding other people, stopping the ball to avoid collisions. Drop and 'catch'.	Rolling through targets using hands.	Rolling using two hands and one hand aiming for accuracy. Stance, sending actions.	As L2. Retrieving a rolling ball. Retrieving a rolling ball.	Using feet. Using hands.
L4	Walking keeping a ball under control with a padder bat.	Grip, using ropes as 'guides'.	Throwing into targets, using hands, underarm.	Aiming for accuracy. Stance, sending actions, working alongside a partner.	Retrieving a rolling ball.	Using a bat.
L5	Walking keeping a ball under control using the feet. Walking keeping a ball under control with a padder bat.	Avoiding other people, stopping the ball to avoid collisions. Grip, using ropes as 'guides'.	As L4.		As L4.	
L6	Jogging, springy jumps over ropes.	Small jumps, safe landings, two feet to two feet.	Rolling ball into a hoop. Rolling to push a cone.	Gentle accurate rolling (judgement of force). Accurate aiming.		
L7	Jogging, springy jumps over ropes. Following a partner.	Small jumps, safe landings, one foot to two feet. Staying close, leading away from collisions.	As L6.			

Reception: scheme of work cont.

	Travelling with/ without equipment	Intended learning outcomes P of S	Sending skills	Intended learning outcomes P of S	Receiving skills	Intended learning outcomes P of S
L8	Springy jumps over ropes, carrying a ball. Following a partner, carrying a ball.	Small jumps, safe landings, one foot to two feet. Co-operation, staying close, leading away from collisions.	Throwing through the air with a bounce.	Accurate aiming into a target, two-handed using different balls.	Receiving from a bounce with a partner.	Stopping, trapping the ball, development of anticipation.
L9	Jogging carrying a ball.	Bounce and catch.	Sending the ball downwards. Sending through a target.	In order to catch it after the bounce: timing of release, judgement of force, overarm action. Slow sending.	Catch from a bounce. Receiving a rolling ball.	Downward cradle, anticipation using two hands, partner activity.
L10			Playing games, a variety of sending skills.	Co-operation alongside or with a partner.	Playing games.	Variety of receiving skills, hands/feet/bat.
L11	Travelling changing speed.	Walk, jog, run.	Sending rolling and with a bounce.	One and two hands, stance	As L9.	
L12	Travelling changing speed. Carrying a ball; putting it down and picking it up.	Walk, jog, run carrying a ball. Partner co-operation, looking for spaces.	As L11.		As L9.	
L13	Moving around the space, keeping a ball under control with a padder bat.	Grip, stopping, push to right and left.	Sending through the air.	Underarm or overarm action.		
L14	As Lesson 13. Dodging game.		As L13.			
L15	As L14.		Playing simple games using a variety of sending skills.	Co-operation and competition alongside or with a partner. Planning and evaluating simple games and beginning to use 'rule structures'.	Playing games.	Variety of receiving skills, hands/feet/bat.

Assessment lesson. Place the equipment in the corners. Divide the children into groups (Red, Blue, Green and Yellow) and introduce them to the different types of equipment.

Red   Blue

Green   Yellow

A. Collect a beanbag and place the beanbag on the floor in a space. Go on a big journey, walking. Do not bump into anyone else. When I say 'Stop' walk to a beanbag of your colour group.

Repeat this several times. Increase the length of the journey. Use curving pathways (putting objects such as beanbags, cones and quoits on the floor 'organises' the space so that curving pathways are easily seen).

Let the children progress from walking to jogging.

B. Collect a quoit or a hoop. Put the quoit/hoop over your beanbag. Pick up your beanbag and hold it in both hands.
    Travel around the space (walking or jogging).

Let the children progress to using one hand (preferred/dominant first, then non-dominant). Ask them to dodge. This will involve making many decisions about safe spaces as they travel.

C. I am going to ask you to give your beanbag to someone else and take theirs. Jog around the space and when I say 'Swap' give your beanbag to someone close to you in exchange for theirs. Then carry on jogging.

Co-operation assessment task. The children should be very close to each other when they swap. In later lessons the 'swap' can be progressed to the concept of a 'pass'.

Red   Blue

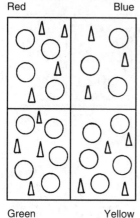

Green   Yellow

A. Collect a hoop/cone or rope. Place it in a big space. Make the ropes into circles, like the hoops. Travel around visiting as many 'hoops'/cones as you can until I say 'Stop'.

Use 'Go' and 'Stop' signals to establish careful listening. Encourage use of all the space and curving pathways (dodging and weaving). Take it slowly at first because children have to watch each other and the objects on the floor – quite a challenge!

B. Collect a ball from your colour corner and stand near a hoop or cone. Using your hands, send the ball to try to hit the hoop/cone. Collect your ball and try again.

If the children succeed ask them to try to make the task harder (see A Progression, page 5). If they miss ask them to make the task easier and then harder again by varying the distance, size of target, type of ball, and doing one- or two-handed roll. This 'aiming' task will enable you to assess stance, one-handed and two-handed, and teach the children by demonstration/ evaluation.

C. Travel around the space carrying your ball in two hands. When you get to a hoop or cone drop the ball and then collect, catch or retrieve it. Continue to other hoops, cones or ropes.

This task will enable you to assess how the children cope with simple 'bounce and catch'. This is a skill which takes a long time to acquire because it involves anticipation ... different balls behave in different ways!

A. Collect a medium/large ball and stand in a space. Put
the ball by your feet. Move around keeping the ball very
close to your feet.

**Experiment with medium/large balls because small
ones will be too difficult to control. Emphasise slow
control using the inside part of the feet. Children will
move around watching the ball and *not* each other.
Expect collisions and then teach the children to stop
the ball when they see another person coming. Most
will use hands to stop the ball. This is fine; trapping
with the feet is a progression. This task can be used
regularly as a concluding activity; repetition builds up
confidence.**

B. Collect two cones/quoits/beanbags. Place them two
paces apart. Roll the ball with your hands through the
cones; retrieve and try again.

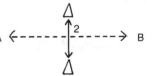

**Emphasise the skills learned in the previous session.
Start with a 'wide' space. Allow children to set their
own challenges, by changing the ball and the distance
they stand away from the target. This will give them a
foundation of experience of how to send, rolling with
accuracy, one- or two-handed, left- and right-handed.**

C. Leave the obstacles in the space. Travel around the
space using your hands to control the ball on the floor
and rolling the ball through the target gaps.

**Let the children begin walking slowly, using both
hands to guide the ball around other people and
through the cones. Praise close control and looking up
to check other people in the space.**

A. Collect any sort of ball. Can you make it move into a space using your hands or feet, jog after it and stop it with your hands or feet? Practise this.

Encourage gentle rolling or 'pushing' with the foot. Allow experimentation with different ways of using hands, e.g. two hands, from between the legs or from the side of the body and front or side of foot and ask the children 'What happened when you . . . ?' 'Can you make it go . . . ?' 'Can you use . . . ?'

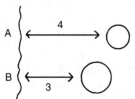

B. Organisation: Green and Yellow groups continue with Activity **A**. Demonstrate Activity **B(i)** to Blue and Red groups. Then demonstrate Activity **B(ii)** to Green and Yellow groups.

B(i) With a partner (or in threes). Equipment: one beanbag/quoit and one hoop each. Send your beanbag or quoit into the hoops.

Underarm sending. Look for backswing and follow through with correct release point. Encourage correct sideways stance for the hand being used. Co-operation alongside a partner.

Safety: make sure all the beanbags are thrown before the children retrieve them.

B(ii) Take a padder bat. Travel slowly around your space using the bat to keep the ball under control. Change your ball if you want to.

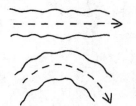

Progress to setting up ropes to guide/challenge the children (see diagram). Teach the correct grip high up the handle of the bat.

C. Briefly show the other half of the class your activity. Then put away your equipment safely.

A. Collect a large/medium ball and stand in a space. Put the ball by your feet. Move around slowly, keeping the ball very close to your feet.

Repetition practice activity. Ask the children to concentrate on close control at walking pace and stopping the ball before colliding with other balls or people. Remember this is a difficult task so ask the children to look up sometimes as they dribble.

B. Let Red and Blue groups continue with Activity **A**.

Demonstrate Activity **B(i)** Lesson 4 to Yellow and Green groups.

Intervene to increase/decrease distance, as necessary. Emphasise safety and praise co-operation.

Demonstrate Activity **B(ii)** Lesson 4 to Red and Blue groups.

Progress to using cones/beanbags to dribble around (see diagram). Ask the children to make the challenge more difficult.

C. Put the equipment away safely in your colour corners.

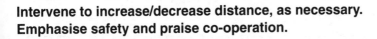

31

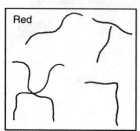

A. Place ropes in your colour space in all sorts of patterns. Jog around and when you come to a rope make a small springy jump over the rope and land well.

You will probably see two-foot to two-foot jumping. Emphasise the use of springy safe landings using the ankles and knees as bendy shock absorbers.

Safety: discourage longer jumps; praise small springy jumps.

B. Organisation: Green and Yellow groups continue with **A**.

Demonstrate Activity **B(i)** to Red and Blue groups. Then demonstrate Activity **B(ii)** to Green and Yellow groups.

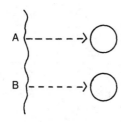

B(i)   With a partner. Equipment: one rope, two hoops, two balls each. Try to roll your ball so that it gets 'trapped' in the hoop.

Very slow rolling and accuracy needed. Ropes can also be used to provide the 'trap'. A variety of balls can be used. Progress from light foam types to airflow and then larger ones.

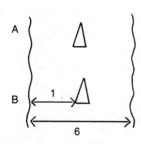

B(ii)   With a partner. Equipment: two ropes, two cones, two medium balls. Roll your ball at the cone so that you push the cone past the rope. Retrieve the ball and try again.

Again rolling accuracy is needed. Two-handed or one-handed action. The children share the space but have a cone each. They must retrieve the ball after each roll. If the cones are weighted use skittles and then knock down.

C. Briefly show the other half of the class your activity.

A. Place ropes in your colour space in all sorts of patterns. Jog around and when you come to a rope make a small springy jump over the rope and land well. (Repetition of Lesson 6.)

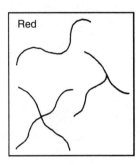

Teach one- to two-footed jumping. Commonsense tells us that some of these footwork patterns are maturational: regress to two-footed to two-footed or jog then stop, stand on one foot, jump over rope, land on two feet. Praise springy safe landings.

B. Let Red and Blue groups continue with Activity **A**.

Demonstrate Activity **B(i)** Lesson 6 to Green and Yellow groups.

Let the children experiment with making the game harder or easier for themselves. Alternatively, cones can be turned on their side and the balls rolled into them (see diagram opposite).

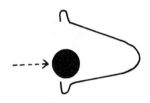

Demonstrate Activity **B(ii)** Lesson 6 to Red and Blue groups.

Children can adjust the cones or the ropes to make the 'game' easier or harder. They can play independently alongside each other or co-operate.

C. Find a partner. One of you is the leader and one is the follower. The follower has to stay close to the leader. When I say 'Go' the leader walks around the space.

Children can also play in threes. Change leader often. Progress to jogging. Praise remaining close and leading away from collisions.

A. Place ropes in your colour space in all sorts of patterns. Collect a medium/large ball. Carry the ball in two hands. When you get to a rope jump over it and make a safe springy landing.

No hands to help balance now! Encourage the children to experiment with holding the ball close to the body, out in front, to the side and under one arm. Which is the best for them?

B. With a partner. Equipment: one hoop, two ropes, one ball. Practise throwing the ball through the air so that it bounces in the hoop. Your partner collects the ball and throws it back in the same way to bounce in the hoop.

Encourage different types of _two-handed_ throwing. Slinging underarm from the side of the body or from between the legs or from overhead. Praise accuracy, using both hands and co-operation.

Children can progress the game themselves by:
- **using different types of ball**
- **changing the distance.**

C. Collect any sort of ball. Find a partner. One of you is the leader and one is the follower. The follower has to stay close to the leader. When I say 'Go' the leader walks around the space.

Praise partner co-operation. Children can carry a ball of their choice.

Once partner work has been introduced 'receiving' can be dealt with as a specific focus for concentrating on the anticipatory 'open' skill aspects.

A. Arrange scattered hoops, ropes and cones.

Take a ball which bounces well. Jog around your space carrying the ball. When you come to a hoop/rope circle/cone, bounce the ball and 'catch' it. Continue to the next hoop.

Red   Blue

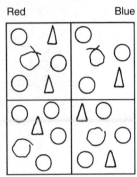

Green   Yellow

Demonstrate sending the ball downwards two-handed so that the ball bounces back directly upwards. Start with the ball at face level and release it at waist height. This 'timing' is important so that the ball can be 'caught'.

The children should use two hands to catch the ball in a 'cradle'. Encourage the children to watch the ball closely all the time so that they can begin to anticipate accurately.

This is a hard task and requires a great deal of practice to master. Regress to drop and catch or to using a slower ball, e.g. large or foam 9 mm ball. Do not allow children to continue if they are not succeeding; move to drop and catch. Drop will give a direct down/up bounce which is best for beginning catchers since it is a trajectory that is easy to anticipate. Start catching with this task because it is easier to follow the flight of the ball from a bounce than it is from a very variable upward toss into the air of a beanbag or ball.

B. With a partner. Equipment: two ropes, beanbags (quoits or cones). Roll the ball to your partner through the cones, etc. Receiver stops the ball in any way with two hands.

Keep the cones, etc. about two paces apart. Insist on slow sending to give the receiver time to make the anticipatory decision (when and where the ball will

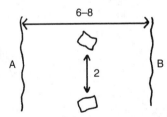

6–8

A   2   B

arrive) and to get the hands into position. The game is played on the feet, *not* sitting or kneeling, because children will need good footwork to move to where the ball goes. Praise the downward cradling action to receive the ball and co-operation.

C. With a partner (or in threes). One ball between two/three. One leader and one follower. The leader carries the ball. When I say 'Change' the leader stops and gives the ball to the follower, who then leads, etc.

Develop from walking quickly to jogging using curving pathways. Progress to using drop/catch to 'pass' the ball to the follower.

A. Choose any piece of apparatus. Travel around the space keeping the apparatus under control.

Limited choice activity. Encourage children to experiment with a variety of apparatus.

B. With a partner. Choose any of the 'games' we have played. Take your equipment into a space and start.

The children can change equipment. They can play alongside each other or co-operate with each other. They should be able to show you *how* their game is played. Allow them some time to modify the 'game'. Intervene in the choice of equipment, the body parts used, and to point out safety aspects.

C. Groups can show each other the games they have played.

The emphasis in this lesson is on:
- *Planning* – **choosing and setting out equipment, body parts to use and how the 'game' will be played; e.g. trying to beat a score**

and
- *Evaluating* – **explaining to the teacher the planning choices – describing how the 'game' is being played.**
- *Teacher's role* – **intervening in appropriate 'choices'.**
  - **Safety – especially in where equipment is set out.**
  - **Helping in 'modifying games', sometimes towards simple competition.**

A.   Go and stand in a space of your own. When I say 'Walk', 'Jog', or 'Run' follow instructions. Be careful not to bump into anyone else. Ready ... 'Jog'.

Change instructions regularly. This change of speed activity is good for warm ups because it is very active and can be used to show children the effects exercise has on their body. For example ask: Are you breathing faster? Do you feel warmer? Do you know why this happens?

B.   Demonstrate Activity **B(i)** to Red and Blue groups, and then Activity **B(ii)** to Green and Yellow groups.

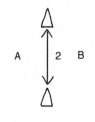

B(i)   With a partner. Equipment: ropes, beanbags/ quoits/cones, ball. Roll the ball to your partner through the cones, etc. Receiver stops the ball in any way with two hands.

As Lesson 9 Activity B. Progress to using different types of ball and use feet and bats as well as hands to send with.

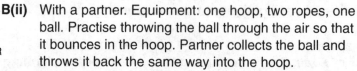

B(ii)   With a partner. Equipment: one hoop, two ropes, one ball. Practise throwing the ball through the air so that it bounces in the hoop. Partner collects the ball and throws it back the same way into the hoop.

As Lesson 8 Activity B. Encourage the children to focus on helping the receiver stop/trap the ball. Keep the hoop close to the sender (see diagram opposite); encourage underarm and overarm sending.

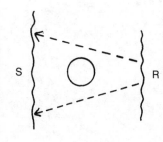

Praise the receivers if they stop or catch the ball because they have made the correct anticipatory decision, then teach them the best way to hold their hands.

Progress to asking the receiver to send the ball back to either side of the hoop.

C.   Briefly show the other half of the class your activity.

A. Go and stand in a space of your own. When I say 'Walk', 'Jog', or 'Run' follow instructions. Be careful not to bump into anyone else. Ready . . . 'Walk'.

Progress this activity so that the children carry a ball as they travel around.

B. Demonstrate Activity **B(ii)** Lesson 11 to Red and Blue groups.

Demonstrate Activity **B(i)** Lesson 11 to Green and Yellow groups.

If a rebound wall is available children can play using similar targets near to the wall (see diagram). Using aiming targets makes the receivers' decisions easier because they are more predictable. This means greater success!

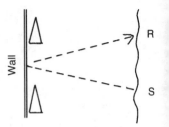

C. With a partner. One leads, the other follows.

The leader has a ball. Jog around, when I clap my hands the leader puts the ball on the floor and the follower picks it up. Continue.

Start by walking and progress to jogging. Use different types of ball or beanbag or quoit. Praise leaders who look for big open spaces!

39

A. Take a small/medium ball and a padder bat, and stand in a space. Put the ball on the floor. Move around, gently patting the ball. Try to keep the ball as close to the bat as you can.

Check for grip high up the handle of the bat. Ask the children to stop the ball using the bat. Encourage them to look up regularly as they move around. This is a slow-walking activity. Most children will keep their heads down and not have the ability to avoid others. Some collisions and loss of control will be inevitable!

B. Organisation: Yellow and Green groups continue Activity **A**.

Demonstrate Activity **B(i)** to Red and Blue groups and then Activity **B(ii)** to Yellow and Green groups.

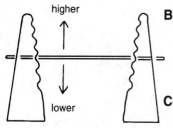

B(i) With a partner. Over/under game. Equipment: skittles/cones, ropes or canes, one medium/large ball. Throw the ball *over* the rope/cane to your partner. Partner returns the ball *under* the rope/cane.

Concentrate on sending accuracy: one-/two-handed.

Receiver traps/stops/catches the ball and sends it back with hands or foot. Change sender/receiver roles.

Let the children suggest ways of developing (harder/easier) the game.

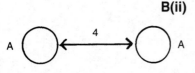

B(ii) With a partner. Equipment: two beanbags, two hoops. Throw the beanbag into your partner's hoop. If you can do this move the hoops one pace further apart.

This is a throw for accuracy game. The children can send underarm or overarm. Teach accuracy of sending. Stance sideways with non-throwing arm pointing in direction of 'target'. Check that the correct foot is forward – the opposite one to the throwing hand.

Develop: ropes can be used instead of hoops.

Differentiation can be built in by making the spaces to aim into wider for less accurate throwers and narrower for the more successful (see diagrams opposite).

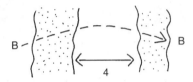

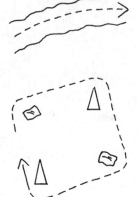

A. Take a small/medium ball and a padder bat and stand in a space. Put the ball on the floor. Move around, gently patting the ball. Try to keep the ball as close to the bat as you can.

Repetition of Activity A Lesson 13. Progress to putting objects in the space for children to dribble round. Demonstrate a 'course', then let children set up their own or share other people's.

B. Organisation: Red and Blue groups continue Activity **A**.

Demonstrate Activity **B(ii)** Lesson 13 to Green and Yellow groups.

Demonstrate **B(i)** Lesson 13 to Red and Blue groups.

C. Put the apparatus away and then find a space. Jog around dodging other people. When I say 'Stations' you must run to your colour corner and stand in a line/circle/holding hands, etc.

Footwork listening game. Check listening concentration by using other words that begin with 'St...'

Safety: ensure children are clear of walls, edges of playgrounds, etc.

A. Play 'Stations'.

As Activity C Lesson 14.

Safety: play in a defined area. Ensure children are clear of walls, windows and the edges of playgrounds. Insist on skilful dodging, not running at full speed.

B. With a partner. Choose any equipment and play a 'game' which we have played before.

Repetition and progression of Lesson 10 (refer to Lesson 10).

The children can change equipment. They can play alongside each other or co-operate with each other.

They should be able to show you *how* their game is played. Allow the children some time to 'modify' the 'game'. Intervene in the choice of equipment, the body parts used, and to ensure safety aspects.

Ask the children if they have any 'rules' by which they play their game. For example, 'What equipment did you decide on?' 'How did you start the game?' 'What do you have to do – roll? Bounce?' 'Where do you aim?'

Show some examples of games to groups in turn. Do not overdo this because the fun is in playing with and against each other.

Year 1: Scheme of work. Many of the activities from Reception are revisited and extended.

	Travelling with/ without equipment	Intended learning outcomes P of S	Sending skills	Intended learning outcomes P of S	Receiving skills	Intended learning outcomes P of S
L1	Jogging around the space. Jogging carrying a ball, two hands and one hand.	Using curving pathways, avoiding other people and obstacles. Stopping skills, revisit springy jumps.	Sending towards a target, using hands, rolling.	Aiming for accuracy, making the task easier or harder. Evaluation of performance, stance, sending actions.	Retrieving a rolling ball.	Using hands.
L2	As L1 plus changing hands. Control using the feet.	Avoiding other people, stopping the ball to avoid collisions.	Bounce and catch.	One-hand, two-hand receive.	Catching from a bounce.	Using two hands, downward cradle.
L3	With a partner, jogging carrying a ball.	Exchanging the ball, using space safely.	Rolling using hands, underarm. Sending using a bounce.	Aiming for accuracy, stance, sending actions, working with a partner. Downward cradle to receive, with a partner.	Retrieve from self roll. Receiving a rolling ball. Moving 'into line'. Catching from a bounce.	Downward cradle action. Using two hands, partner activity. Anticipation of where the ball will arrive. With a partner, downward cradle.
L4	Control using the feet. With a partner, jogging carrying a ball.	Stopping the ball with the bottom of the foot. Exchanging the ball, using bounces.	Sending with feet. Sending using a bounce.	Accuracy, through gaps, different parts of foot. With a partner.	Catching from a bounce.	With a partner, downward cradle.
L5	Walking keeping a ball under control with a padder bat. Dribbling using padder bat. Jogging with partner.	Grip, stopping/ trapping, looking up to avoid collisions. Moving the ball with accuracy through gaps. Put down and pick up practice.	Sending with bat.	Accuracy, through gaps, both sides of bat.	Trapping with a bat. Picking up a ball from the floor.	Using both sides of the bat. 'Forehand and backhand' sides.

Year 1: Scheme of work. Many of the activities from Reception are revisited and extended. *cont.*

	Travelling with/without equipment	Intended learning outcomes P of S	Sending skills	Intended learning outcomes P of S	Receiving skills	Intended learning outcomes P of S
L6	Games making.	All footwork skills.	Playing games.	Variety of sending skills. Planning, Performing and Evaluating, rule structures.	Catch from a downward bounce. Playing games.	Downward cradle, anticipation. Variety of receiving skills, hands/feet/bat co-operation and competition, explanation of game.
L7	Jogging carrying a ball in one hand on the palm. Carrying a ball.	Looking forward while travelling. Throw up, bounce and retrieve/catch.	Throwing a ball into the air.	Upwards for accuracy, stationary, progressing to walking.	Catch from an upward throw.	After one bounce, downward cradle stationary and moving.
L8	Carrying a ball.	Throw up, bounce and retrieve/catch using downward cradle.	Sending the ball with many bounces. Throwing the ball into a hoop.	Accurately to partner, two-handed, one-handed. With one bounce.	As L7. Receiving after a bounce.	From a partner, anticipation.
L9	Travelling with a ball at feet around obstacles. Travelling carrying a ball with partner following.	Increased difficulty with obstacles and people to monitor. Bounce and catch.	As L8.	Differentiation of tasks.	Receiving after a bounce.	From a partner, anticipation, progression to moving into line.
L10	Travelling with ball at feet.	Trapping the ball on command.	Sending rolling. Kicking.	One and two hands, stance for accuracy, different parts of foot.	Stopping the ball with feet. Trapping the ball with feet.	While moving, bottom of foot. Receiving from a partner.
L10	As L11. Pass the Braid.	Further practice of trapping a moving ball. Dodging/chasing.	As L10.		As L10.	

Year 1: Scheme of work. Many of the activities from Reception are revisited and extended. *cont.*

	Travelling with/without equipment	Intended learning outcomes P of S	Sending skills	Intended learning outcomes P of S	Receiving skills	Intended learning outcomes P of S
L12			Bouncing the ball with a bat. Trap and hit with bat.	Drop and hit, competition against self. Hitting along ground for accuracy.		
L13	Jogging, bounce and catch.	Dodging and weaving, using space safely.	Hitting a ball to partner. Throwing into a target.	Hitting with hand/bat after bounce. Scoring system, competition.	Retrieve/catch/stop.	From a ball which is hit.
L14	Change the Ball.	Carrying the ball, dodging/chasing.	As L13.		As L13	
L15			Playing games. A variety of sending skills.	Co-operation with a partner/competition. Planning, Performing and Evaluating. Developing and explaining simple rules.	As L6.	Rule structure progression, evaluation skills.

46

A. Collect a cone, quoit or beanbag. Place it on the floor in a space. Jog around and stop on the signal. Use all the space.

Encourage children to travel on the front part of their feet (ball of foot). Check for safe controlled stopping, bending knees, using front leg as a 'brake'. Progress to revising springy jumps (see Reception Lessons 6 and 7).

B. Collect a small/medium ball. Hold the ball in two hands. Jog around and stop on the signal.

Encourage use of curving pathways, with lots of dodging and making decisions. Progress to carrying the ball in one hand (dominant then non-dominant).

C. Roll the ball, aiming to hit your cone, quoit or beanbag. If you are successful make the task harder for yourself. If you miss make the task easier.

Encourage rolling using two hands and one hand, or foot. Padder bat or unihoc stick can be introduced.

To make this activity harder: increase distance, use smaller target, smaller ball, change body part/equipment used, use non-dominant hand or foot.

To make this activity easier: decrease distance, use larger target, larger ball, use two hands, check stance for aiming.

A. Collect a cone, quoit or beanbag and a small/medium ball. Put the cone/quoit/beanbag in a space. Jog around carrying the ball in one hand. Change hands when I say 'Change'.

When children change the ball from one hand to the other they need to 'monitor' the change by looking at their hands and therefore are not looking where they are going. Progress to teaching them to look ahead all the time and still be able to 'see' their hands.

B. Jog around carrying the ball in one hand. When you get to a cone, etc., bounce the ball downwards and catch it in *two* hands.

Teach the downward sending action so that the ball bounces directly upwards: bent elbow, 'two-finger' grip, ball held by side of head and released by the knee. Some children will send with two hands if they have a medium ball and catch with two. Some will drop and catch the ball.

Progress all children to a smaller ball – use slow-bouncing foam ones for the less advanced and tennis-type balls for children who can cope with a faster, higher bounce.

Focus on the accuracy of the sending action *not* the catch at this stage. Praise any type of getting the hands near to the ball to 'trap' it.

C. Put the ball at your feet. Travel slowly around the whole space, keeping the ball very close to your feet. If you see you are going to bump into someone else, stop your ball and then move away into a space.

Children can change their ball if what they here is not suitable for dribbling. Encourage them to look up regularly as they travel and to use the inside of *both* feet.

A. Take any sort of ball. Stand in a space. Roll the ball
gently into a space, overtake the ball and let it roll into
your hands.

**Ask the children to use a downward cradle action to
collect the ball. Insist on smooth gentle rolling into a
free space. Check the sideways stance. Encourage lots
of rolling and retrieving to make the children active ...
'How many can you do before...'**

Allow children to change the ball or use a quoit.

B. With a partner. Collect two cones/beanbags/quoits, and
one ball. Place the cones/beanbags/quoits about two
paces apart. Roll the ball to each other through the
cones.

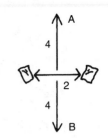

**Ask the children to use a downward cradle to stop the
ball and to keep about four paces back from the cones
so that they have enough time to anticipate where the
ball will arrive. Ask the receiver to watch the sender's
hand as the ball is released so that he/she can make an
early decision as to where the ball will arrive.**

**If successful, the cones, etc. can be moved further
apart and the sender asked to send the ball to the *side*
of the receiver. The receiver then has to move to the
right or left to stop the ball. This is called 'moving into
line behind the ball'.**

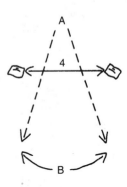

C. Put the cones, etc. away; keep the ball. One partner
leads and the other follows. The leader carries the ball.
The follower tries to stay close to the leader. Jog and
when I say 'Change' the leader turns and bounces the
ball for the follower to 'catch'. Follower now leads.
Continue.

Praise co-operation and rapid changeovers.

A. Take a medium ball and dribble the ball with your feet. Try to keep the ball close to your feet. Move slowly.

Encourage use of all the space because learners need room to make mistakes and many will look down at their feet, ignoring others in the space. Encourage them to stop the ball regularly to look up. Ask them to stop the ball with the bottom of their feet. This practice takes a long time to perfect. Most children will stop the ball with their hands.

B. Collect two cones/beanbags/quoits and place them in your colour grid about two paces apart. Dribble the ball through the gaps between the cones, etc. You may use all the space.

Encourage the children to use the insides of both feet to move the ball. The children have to look up to spot the gaps. Progress to making some gaps smaller.

C. Put the cones, etc. away; keep the ball. One partner leads and the other follows. The leader carries the ball. The follower tries to stay close to the leader. Jog and when I say 'Change' the leader turns and bounces or rolls the ball for the follower to 'catch'. The follower now leads. Continue.

Some children will use several bounces to their partner. Progress to one bounce then catch. Praise co-operation and rapid changeovers.

A. Take a medium/small ball and a padder bat. Dribble the
ball with your bat. Try to keep the ball very close to
your bat. Move slowly at first.

**Use all the space because learners need room to make
mistakes and many will look down at their bat, ignoring
others in the space. Encourage them to stop the ball
regularly to look up. Ask them to stop the ball with one
side of the bat, trapping the ball against the floor.
Some will stop the ball with their hands.**

B. collect two cones/beanbags/quoits and place them in
your colour grid about one pace apart. Dribble the ball
through the gaps between the cones, etc. You may use
all the space.

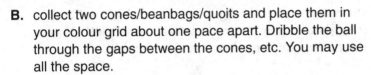

**Ask the children to use both sides of the bat to move
the ball. The children have to look up to spot the gaps.
Progress to making some gaps smaller.**

C. With a partner. One leads the other follows.
The leader has a ball. Jog around; when I clap my
hands the leader puts the ball on the floor and the
follower picks it up. Continue.

**Use different types of ball or beanbag or quoit. Ask the
leaders to dodge and weave. Praise leaders who look
for big open spaces and followers who manage to stay
close.**

A. Choose any piece of equipment and travel around your colour grid keeping the equipment under control.

Note the variation in actions and encourage children to use a variety of equipment or to improve one action.

B. Take a ball which bounces well. How many times can you bounce and catch the ball before I say 'Stop'?

Repeat and try to beat your own score.

Dropping and catching is an acceptable method. Intervene to provide the less advanced with slower-bouncing balls which are easier to catch.

C. With a partner. Collect three cones, four ropes and one ball. Play a rolling game. When I ask you, I want you to be able to explain the game to me.

Intervene only with children who are not following the task or who are in an unsafe space. Ask the children to explain their game: how it works; why they choose . . . ; what they are going to do to improve the game; how they start it. All these things are the 'rules' they are playing by. Take care with groupings: games can be based on friendship or mixed-ability groups. Emphasise co-operation and competition, e.g. against the group's best score (six kicks through the cones). Suggest that the children add equipment which will improve/modify the game.

Note some games to show other groups and to use in other lessons.

A. Collect a small ball from your colour corner. Jog around the grid carrying the ball in one hand.

Now place the ball on your *palm*. Walk around with the ball balanced on the palm of your hand, and when you feel ready begin jogging.

Demonstrate how to 'hold' the ball on the palm. Encourage the children to stretch out their arms so that they can see the ball *and others moving in the space*. Progress to jogging and stopping and starting again, and to using non-dominant hands.

B. Stand in a space in your grid. Hold the ball by your knee, palm upwards. Bring your arm up and release the ball in front of your face so that the ball goes straight up in the air. Let it bounce once and retrieve/catch it. See if you can do this three times/five times . . .

Train the children to watch the ball from the knee to release, then the whole flight of the ball to the catch. In this way they can begin to anticipate where and how the ball will bounce. Begin with low throws and praise upward flight.

Correct children throwing the ball back over their heads; the release point is too late. Regress to a larger ball using two hands to throw the ball.

C. Carry the ball walking around the space. Send the ball a small way upwards and catch/retrieve it after a bounce.

The children now have to learn to 'toss' the ball a little way in front because they are moving. This skill is not easy and requires a lot of practice. Progress to jogging.

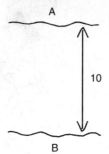

A. Collect a small/medium ball from your colour corner. Stand in a space in your grid.

Carry the ball walking around the space. Send the ball a small way upwards and catch/retrieve it after a bounce.

Repetition of Activity C Lesson 7. Children have to 'throw/toss' the ball a little way in front of them and a short distance into the air. Look for use of two-hand downward cradle for catching.

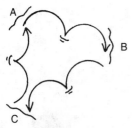

B. Organisation: Green and Yellow groups continue with Activity **A**.

Demonstrate Activity **B(i)** to Blue and Red groups and then demonstrate Activity **B(ii)** to Green and Yellow groups.

B(i)   With a partner (or in threes). You need two ropes about ten paces apart and one ball. Send the ball to your partner. Make the ball bounce many times. Send overarm or underarm.
Make the first bounce close to yourself.

Receiver: should watch the ball from the sender's hand, stop/catch with a downward cradle action.

Progress from larger to smaller ball when ready.

Sender: large ball two-handed overhead; small ball one-handed overarm, using bent elbow.

Introduce a small hoop/rope circle for the senders to aim into to increase number of bounces, because at this stage it is easier to 'track' a number of bounces than flight through the air.

B(ii)   With a partner. You need two hoops/rope circles and one ball. A sends the ball into hoop 1. B catches/stops the ball, and sends it back by bouncing it in hoop 2.

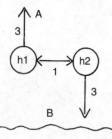

Sender and receiver teaching points as in B(i). The children should stand about 3 paces from the hoops. If necessary, put in ropes to guide players.

C. Briefly show the other half of the class your activity. Then put the equipment away carefully.

A. Place cones, skittles, and quoits/beanbags in your colour grid. Collect a large/medium ball and place it at your feet. Travel around keeping the ball very close to your feet.

Encourage the children to look up regularly to spot obstacles and other people in the space. Encourage the use of both feet and different parts of the foot to move/control/stop the ball.

B. Organisation: Blue and Red groups continue with Activity **A**.

Demonstrate Activity **B(i)** Lesson 8 to Green and Yellow groups.

Progress to sender aiming to the side of the receiver (see diagram). This makes the receiver watch the sender's action more closely in order to anticipate where the ball will arrive and then to 'move into line' (see Activity B Lesson 3).

Demonstrate Activity **B(ii)** lesson 8 to Red and Blue groups.

Progress to A and B choosing which hoop to send into. This makes the receiver watch the sender's action more closely in order to anticipate where the ball will arrive, and then to 'move into line' (see Activity B Lesson 3).

Further progression:
● **move hoops two paces apart**
● **move hoops closer to sender and receiver**
● **children choose where to place hoops.**

C. Put the hoops, etc. away; keep the ball. One partner leads and the other follows. The leader carries the ball. The follower tries to stay close to the leader. Jog and when I say 'Change' the leader turns and bounces the ball for the follower to catch. The follower now leads. Continue.

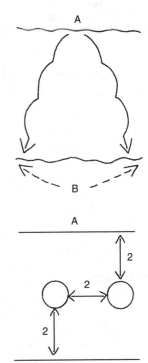

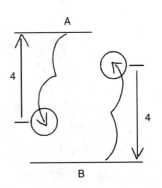

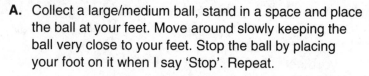

A. Collect a large/medium ball, stand in a space and place the ball at your feet. Move around slowly keeping the ball very close to your feet. Stop the ball by placing your foot on it when I say 'Stop'. Repeat.

To stop the ball the children need to be able to balance on one foot. This requires a lot of practice and should be done slowly. If the ball runs away the children can collect it with their hands.

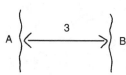

B. Organisation: Red and Blue groups continue with Activity **A**, stopping the ball when they 'meet' other people.

Demonstrate Activity **B(i)** to Green and Yellow groups and then demonstrate Activity **B(ii)** to Red and Blue groups.

B(i) With a partner. Equipment: one ball, two ropes. A rolls the ball underarm to B. B traps the ball with his/her foot and sends the ball back to A for A to trap. Continue.

Encourage the children to trap the ball with the bottom of the foot, in a 'wedge' shape. You may see some children use the side of their foot. Rolling should be slow to allow the receiver time to get ready.

B(ii) With a partner. Equipment: one ball, two cones. A kicks the ball to B through the cones. B stops the ball with his/her hands and sends the ball back to A with his/her foot.

Encourage the children to use different parts of the foot to strike the ball, the inside and front for example. The ball should be at the side of and just in front of the *non-kicking foot*.

C. Briefly show the other half of the class your activity.

56

A. Collect a large/medium ball, stand in a space and place the ball at your feet. Move around slowly keeping the ball very close to your feet. Stop the ball by placing your foot on it when I say 'Stop'. Repeat.

Repetition of Lesson 10 Activity A.

B. Organisation: Green and Yellow groups continue Activity **A**.

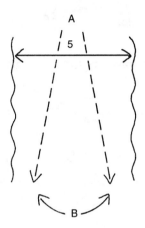

Demonstrate Activity **B(i)** Lesson 10 to Red and Blue groups.

Progress to sender rolling the ball to the side of the receiver. Widen the ropes to 4/5 paces apart. The receiver must 'move into line' after 'reading' the sender's actions. Direct the receiver's attention to the sender's hand.

Demonstrate Activity **B(ii)** Lesson 10 to Green and Yellow groups.

If the children are not achieving success widen the gap between the cones. This is a difficult skill which will not be mastered in one day.

C. As a contrast, play Pass the braid. About eight to ten of you will be catchers wearing a braid. When touched by a catcher, the caught person takes the braid and becomes the catcher.

Restrict the space and encourage dodging rather than dangerous speed. Play away from walls, windows and playground edges.

A. Put cones/beanbags/quoits/hoops in your space. Collect a small/medium ball and a padder bat. Hit the ball gently with the bat to hit a cone, etc. Start close to a 'target'. Retrieve the ball and aim again.

Some children could use hands and then change over. Ensure sideways stance (as in underarm rolling). See that the children's grip is as if shaking hands with the bat, i.e. right up the handle. (If using hand, children should use an open palm.) Ask the children to watch what happens to the ball, and tell you about what happens (evaluation).

B(i) Drop the ball from waist height and try to bounce it once with the bat. Collect the ball and try again. Can you do two or three bounces? Can you do more?

Encourage use of stiff wrist and forearm. Movement is from the shoulder and the bat face should be kept parallel to the floor. Demonstrate this. Use slower foam balls to begin with for children losing control.

While Red and Blue groups continue the above activity, introduce Activity **B(ii)** to Green and Yellow groups.

B(ii) With a partner. Equipment: two cones, one ball, one bat each. Roll the ball to your partner through the cones. Partner traps the ball with his/her bat or hand and hits the ball back through the gap. Make the game harder when you can play it well.

Stop Red and Blue groups and show them the game being played. Send them off to get organised and play.

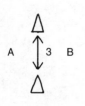

A   3   B

Teaching points as Activity A for striking the ball gently. Receiver stops the ball with the bat *before* returning it.

C. Return to Activity **B(i)**. Beat your own best score.

This is a difficult skill. Children need a suitable ball and lots of practice.

A. Put cones/beanbags/quoits/hoops in your space. Collect a small/medium ball. Jog around carrying the ball in one hand and when you come to a cone, etc. bounce the ball by the cone, catch it, and continue to the next one.

One-handed overarm sending and two-handed catching. Ask the children 'How many cones can you visit before I say...'

B. Organisation: Red and Blue groups continue Activity **A**.

Demonstrate Activity **B(i)** to Green and Yellow groups and then demonstrate Activity **B(ii)** to Red and Blue groups.

B(i)　With a partner. Equipment: one padder bat, one hoop, one small ball. A drops the ball, from waist height, into the hoop and after the bounce hits it gently to B. B rolls the ball back to A. Change over after three hits.

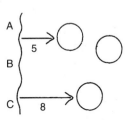

The children should hold the bat in backswing position, then drop the ball and try to strike it. The timing of the hit is not easy and at first it is better to use a foam ball rather than a tennis ball because the foam ball bounces more slowly and travels less far when hit.

B(ii)　Equipment: beanbags, hoops/rope circles. Throw the beanbags into targets.

The children can invent a scoring system. Teach overarm throwing, starting with a bent elbow, sideways stance, and pointing at the target with the _non-throwing_ hand. If the right hand is used for throwing check that the left foot is forward, and the opposite for left-handed throwers.

Safety: both partners should throw all the beanbags before any are retrieved.

A. Play Change the ball: about eight to ten of you will be catchers with braids but no ball and the rest will have a ball each to carry. When touched by a catcher, the caught person takes the braid and the catcher takes the ball.

Restrict the space; play in four grids (half a netball court).

Safety: beware of walls, windows and playground edges, etc. Discourage speed and encourage dodging.

B. Organisation: Green and Yellow groups continue Activity **A**.

Demonstrate Activity **B(i)** Lesson 13 to Red and Blue groups and then demonstrate Activity **B(ii)** Lesson 13 to Green and Yellow groups.

Let the children adjust distance to hoops and develop scoring systems which they can explain.

C. Play Change the ball again, but this time carry one piece of equipment of your choice (bat/quoit/cone, etc.).

A. Free choice of travelling with a piece of equipment
keeping the equipment under control.

**Encourage use of different body parts and intervene to
improve individual skills.**

B. With a partner (or in threes) play a passing game. Use
a variety of equipment.

**Allow the children a choice of equipment.
Intervene in the spacing of the 'game' for safety, and
advise on the use of equipment. Ask them to explain to
you how they decided on their game (rule structure)
and how they have changed it.**

Year 2: Scheme of work. Many of the activities from Year 1 are revisited and extended.

	Travelling with/ without equipment	Intended learning outcomes P of S	Sending skills	Intended learning outcomes P of S	Receiving skills	Intended learning outcomes P of S
L1	Travelling controlling the ball with hands and feet.	Avoid other people, stopping the ball to avoid collisions. Using curving pathways.	Throwing a ball into the air, bounce and retrieve/catch. Sending using a bounce.	Upwards for accuracy, stationary assessment task. With a partner, aiming assessment task.	Catching from a bounce. Receiving a rolling ball. Moving 'into line'.	Using two hands, downward cradle. Using two hands, partner activity. Anticipation of where the ball will arrive.
L2	Jogging carrying beanbag in two hands. Walking, throw and catch, dribbling a ball with feet.	Safe stopping action, dodging other people. Tossing beanbag/ quoit a little in front, through 'gaps' accurately.	Throwing a beanbag/ quoit upwards. Rolling with hands.	For accuracy, release point. For accuracy, through gaps.	Catching a beanbag/quoit. Receiving a rolling ball. Moving 'into line'.	From self throw upwards. Using two hands, partner activity. Anticipation of where the ball will arrive, increase in decision making, three cones.
L3	Walking, throw and catch. Dribbling a ball with feet.	Tossing beanbag/ quoit a little in front, watching beanbag/ quoit and other people. Further practice, no obstacles.	Sending a ball with a bounce.	Two- and one-handed actions.	Catching from a bounce.	With a partner, downward cradle, increase in decision making, two hoops.
L4	Jogging and jumping over ropes and in/out of hoops. With a partner, walking and passing a ball.	Safe landings, 1 foot to 2, 2 feet to 2 jumps. Sideways swing pass.	Sending a ball with a bounce. Throwing into a space.	Two- and one-handed actions. Underarm and overarm.	As L3.	
L5	Control using the feet. With a partner, walking and passing a ball.	Stopping the ball with the bottom of the foot, obstacles in the space. Sideways swing pass.	Passing with feet. Rolling with hands.	For accuracy, through gaps.	Receiving a rolling ball with the hands.	From ball which has been kicked.

Year 2: Scheme of work. Many of the activities from Year 1 are revisited and extended. *cont.*

	Travelling with/ without equipment	Intended learning outcomes P of S	Sending skills	Intended learning outcomes P of S	Receiving skills	Intended learning outcomes P of S
L6	Control using the feet. With a partner, dribbling a ball.	Stopping the ball with the bottom of the foot, obstacles in the space. Stopping ball and changing the lead.	Passing with feet.	For accuracy, through gaps, sidefoot pass.	Trapping a ball.	Using feet, moving into line, using boundaries.
L7	With a partner, dribbling a ball. Travelling carrying a ball.	Stopping ball and changing the lead, add short pass. Bounce and catch.	As L6.		As L6.	
L8	With a partner, travelling passing a ball. Playing games.	Sideways swing pass. A variety of footwork skills.	Playing games.	A variety of sending skills, using different body parts and equipment.	Catching a ball passed through the air. Playing games.	Introduction of 'through the air' receiving. A variety of receiving skills.
L9	Travelling with a bat.	Unihoc if available.	Bouncing a ball. Rolling ball using a padder bat. Throwing into a space.	On the spot, attempt more than one bounce. For accuracy, through gaps. Underarm and overarm, rule making.	Trapping with a bat. Catching from a bounce.	Using both sides of the bat, 'forehand and backhand' sides. With a partner, downward cradle.
L10	As L9.		As L9.		As L9.	
L11	Jogging carrying a ball in one hand on the palm. With partner, following.	Looking forward while travelling. Pass beanbag/ball through the air.	Throwing through the air.	For accuracy, underarm.	Receiving through the air.	Increase in distance, more decision making.

Year 2: Scheme of work. Many of the activities from Year 1 are revisited and extended. *cont.*

	Travelling with/without equipment	Intended learning outcomes P of S	Sending skills	Intended learning outcomes P of S	Receiving skills	Intended learning outcomes P of S
L12	Travelling with changes of speed, walk, jog, sprint, stride.	Effects of exercise on the body.	Throwing for distance.	Safety, underarm, sling, overarm. Large and small ball.	Stopping a ball thrown for distance.	Some children can be expected to make the correct decisions and get hands to stop (if not catch) the ball.
L13	Jog, sprint, stride. With a partner.	Acceleration, knee and arm action. Pass a ball through the air.	Rolling with hands.	Making decisions who to send to.	Stopping and picking up the ball.	Game where sending decisions need to be made.
L14	Dodging. Jog, sprint, stride.	Acceleration, knee and arm action.	Rolling to hit moving target.	Making decisions where to send to.	As L13.	
L15	Dodging. Playing games.	A variety of footwork skills.	Playing games.	A variety of sending skills, using different body parts and equipment, rule structure and scoring.	Playing games	A variety of receiving skills.

A. Collect a ball and a beanbag/cone/quoit from your colour corner and go to stand in a space. Travel around the space controlling the ball with your hands or feet.

Assessment practice. Allow children to change the ball to suit the body part being used. Encourage careful travelling, looking up regularly to avoid collisions. Praise stopping with the ball under control.

B. Stand by a cone, etc. Practise throwing the ball into the air. Let the ball bounce once and catch it with two hands.

Assessment task. The ball should be held by the knee and released in front of the face so that it goes directly upwards.

Train the children to watch the ball from knee to release, then the whole flight of the ball to 'catch'. In this way they can begin to anticipate where and how the ball will bounce. Begin with low throws, and praise upward flight.

Correct children throwing the ball back over their heads; the release point is too late. Regress to larger ball using two hands to throw the ball.

C. With a partner. Equipment: one ball, two beanbags/cones/quoits. Roll or bounce the ball through the cones, etc. to your partner.

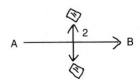

Aiming assessment task. Look for underarm rolling action with sideways stance, and bouncing action using one or two hands depending on size of the ball. Encourage the children to use a downward cradle to receive.

Progress to asking the sender to roll/bounce the ball so that the receiver has to move to the side, 'into line'. Ask the children to make the 'game' harder. Can they think how?

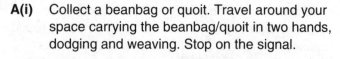

A(i) Collect a beanbag or quoit. Travel around your space carrying the beanbag/quoit in two hands, dodging and weaving. Stop on the signal.

The children should travel on the front part of the feet (ball of foot). Encourage safe controlled stopping, bending knees, using front leg as a 'brake'.

A(ii) Walk around the grid throwing the beanbag/quoit a little way into the air and catching it again. Watch out for other people.

Now the children have to learn to 'toss' the ball a little way in front because they are moving. This skill is not easy and requires a lot of practice. Progress to jogging.

Red and Blue groups continue with Activity **A**. Demonstrate Activity **B** to Yellow and Green groups.

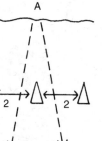

B. Three cone game. Equipment: Two ropes, one ball, three cones/beanbags/quoits. Roll the ball to your partner through the spaces between the cones, etc. Stand behind the rope to receive.

Sender has a choice of where to move receiver, who has to watch sender's hand closely to anticipate where the ball will arrive. Downward cradle to receive.

Demonstrate the Three cone game to Red and Blue groups.

Intervene in the decisions the receivers make. Praise accurate slow rolling to make the game active, it is no fun chasing a ball all the time.

C. Leave the cones in the space. Those who do not have a ball, collect one. Travel around with the ball at your feet, and when you get to a cone 'gap' gently pass the ball through it, retrieve the ball and continue.

Praise slow, controlled footwork, using inside parts of both feet. Children should stop the ball with the bottom of the foot.

A. Walk around the grid throwing a beanbag/ball a little way into the air and catching it again. Watch out for other people.

Repetition of Activity A(ii) Lesson 2. The children have to learn to 'toss' the beanbag a little way in front because they are moving. Progress to slow jogging. Allow the children to change the ball to suit their success. Self evaluation.

B(i)   Green and Yellow groups play the Three cone game as in Activity **B** Lesson 2.

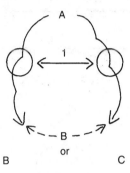

Progress to trying to stop the ball before it crosses the rope and to making the game harder/easier, or using hands and feet.

Demonstrate to Red and Blue groups the Bouncing game.

B(ii)   With a partner (or in threes). Equipment: two hoops/rope circles, one large/medium ball. Bounce the ball into either hoop so that it reaches your partner.

Two-handed overhead sending, downward cradle to receive. Progress to a small ball (foam before tennis type) using one-handed sending (overarm).

Ask the children if they can make the game harder or easier (e.g. by adjusting the hoops).

C. Leave the obstacles out. Conclude briefly with Activity **C** Lesson 2.

Red

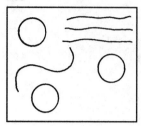

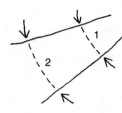

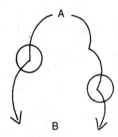

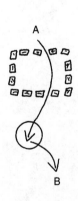

A. Take a hoop or a rope and place it anywhere in your grid. Jog around and when you 'meet' a rope jump over it, and when you get to a hoop jump into and out of it.

Safety: children should not attempt to jump *over* hoops. Beware of hoops sliding on floors or playgrounds, especially if children step on the edges. Teach springy landings with bending knees absorbing the shock. Children can use two-feet to two-feet or one-foot to two-feet landings. Emphasise the use of arms to balance landings.

Place ropes so that they make 'differentiated' challenges (see diagram opposite).

B(i) Yellow and Green play the Bouncing game Activity **B(ii)** Lesson 3.

Two-handed overhead sending, downward cradle to receive. Progress to a small ball (foam before tennis type) using one-handed sending (overarm).

Ask the children if they can make the game harder or easier (e.g. by adjusting the hoops).

Demonstrate Activity **B(ii)** the throwing game to Red and Blue groups.

B(ii) With a partner. Equipment: hoops, ropes, beanbags to mark out circles or squares. A throws a large/ medium ball to land in B's circle. B lets the ball bounce then collects it, and throws it back to land in A's square.

Progress: distance can be increased, ball can be changed for a smaller one. Progress from underarm to overarm throwing. Can the children invent a scoring system?

Safety: Make sure groups do not throw across each other. Not suitable for indoors; needs space.

When appropriate, demonstrate Activity **B(ii)** to Yellow and Green groups.

C. With a partner (or in threes). Equipment: one ball per group, walk around the space passing the ball to each other.

Partners must stay close together. Encourage the children to pass sideways as they move forwards in a straight pathway.

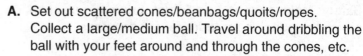

A. Set out scattered cones/beanbags/quoits/ropes. Collect a large/medium ball. Travel around dribbling the ball with your feet around and through the cones, etc.

The ball should be very close to the feet. The children should use mainly the inside of both feet to move the ball; trap the ball with the bottom of the foot to stop it and look up regularly to spot obstacles and other people. Praise co-operation and close control.

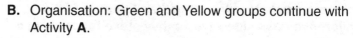

B. Organisation: Green and Yellow groups continue with Activity **A**.

Demonstrate the Three cone passing game, Activity **B(i)** to Red and Blue groups. Then introduce it to Green and Yellow groups.

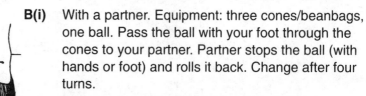

B(i) With a partner. Equipment: three cones/beanbags, one ball. Pass the ball with your foot through the cones to your partner. Partner stops the ball (with hands or foot) and rolls it back. Change after four turns.

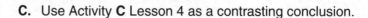

The children should use sidefoot pass, where kicking foot is at 90 degrees to the non-kicking foot. The non-kicking foot points at the target (sideways stance). The kicker bends the knee of the non-kicking leg to 'roll' the ball smoothly along the floor. Young children find kicking a ball whilst balancing on one leg quite a challenge. They need to practise.

C. Use Activity **C** Lesson 4 as a contrasting conclusion.

A. Set out scattered cones/beanbags/quoits/ropes.

Collect a large/medium ball. Travel around dribbling the ball with your feet around and through the cones, etc.

Repetition of Activity A Lesson 5 .

B. All groups play the Three cone passing game (see Activity **B(i)** Lesson 5).

B(i)   Red and Blue groups place boundary ropes at the end of the space. Players must try to stop/trap the ball *before* it crosses the line.

Widen the cone gaps to allow for successful aiming and to make the receiver make decisions! Allow four goes before swapping kicker and roller.

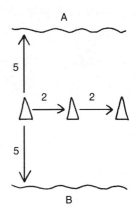

B(ii)   Demonstrate to Yellow and Green groups.

Pass the ball with your foot through the cones to your partner. Partner stops the ball (with hands or foot) and kicks it back.

Use sidefoot pass, where kicking foot is at 90 degrees to the non-kicking foot. The non-kicking foot points at the target (sideways stance). The kicker bends the knee of the non-kicking leg to 'roll' the ball smoothly along the floor. The ball must be stopped/trapped and moved to the correct position to return it with an accurate kick.

C. With a partner (or in threes). One ball between two (or three). A leads dribbling the ball with the feet, B follows. When I say 'Change' A stops the ball for B to take the lead. Continue.

A. With a partner (or in threes). One ball between two (or three). A leads dribbling the ball with the feet, B follows. When I say 'Change' A stops the ball for B to take the lead. Continue.

Repetition and progression of Activity C Lesson 6. Progress to A stopping the ball and making a short pass to B. Praise co-operation and accuracy.

B. Green and Yellow groups continue with Activity **A**, changing when the players decide.

Demonstrate Activity **B(ii)** Lesson 6 to Red and Blue groups.

This time focus the receiver's attention on making accurate decisions. Ask him/her to watch the foot of the sender and to tell you where the ball is going to come. The children can judge this by looking at which way the foot is facing.

Then demonstrate to Yellow and Green groups Activity **B(i)** Lesson 6.

Ask the children to modify this practice to make it harder for themselves. They can change the equipment or introduce a scoring system. Insist on gentle kicking.

C. Take a bouncy ball. Move around bouncing and catching the ball. How many catches can you make? Repeat.

Two-handed or one-handed sending for the bounce. Regress those who are less successful to large or slower foam balls, progress those who are successful to more than one bounce with a larger ball or to faster, smaller balls.

A. With a partner (or in threes). One ball between two (or three). Walk around the space passing the ball to each other.

Partners must stay close together. Encourage them to pass sideways as they move forwards in a straight pathway.

B. With a partner (or in threes). Play a passing game. When you have set up your game try to make it harder for yourselves, e.g. by changing the equipment you play with.

Allow the children a choice of equipment.

Intervene in the spacing of the 'game' for safety, and advise on the use of equipment. Get them to explain to you how they made their game (rule structure) and how they have changed it.

Some groups may be scoring: encourage those children who are co-operating to keep a rally going, and also those who are competing against each other. Intervene to make the competition as *fair* as possible.

Note the games which are working well and have rules, so that you can use them to illustrate what rules are: agreed ways of playing.

A. Take a ball which bounces well. Stand in a space. Bounce the ball as many times as you can.

The children should use their fingertips (not the palm). See that they bend the arm at the elbow and keep the wrist stiff. They should follow the bounce of the ball with the hand down and up instead of 'patting' the ball. Progress to using a smaller ball; regress to using a larger ball, send downwards and catch, drop and catch. This skill needs much practice with the 'best' sort of ball for the learner – a ball that has a consistent bounce so that it behaves the same each time it is bounced.

B. Organisation: Red and Blue groups continue with Activity **A**.

Demonstrate Activity **B(i)** to Green and Yellow groups and then Activity **B(ii)** to Red and Blue groups.

B(i) With a partner. Equipment: three beanbags/cones, etc., one bat each. Send the ball through the cone gaps to your partner.

Look for stopping the ball before it is sent back, and the use of both sides of the bat. Praise children who choose to send the ball away from the receiver, who must then move to intercept it. (Unihoc sticks can be used.)

B(ii) Hand tennis. Throw the ball over the cane/ropes to your partner so that it bounces before it is caught, etc.

Side ropes give the effect of a court boundary. Ask the children to modify the game to suit themselves. Can they invent some rules or scoring system? See diagrams opposite for the two types of equipment that can be used.

C. If there are enough unihoc sticks practise dribbling about the space. If not some of you practise hand-bouncing (try to beat your own record) and some try with a padder bat. This is not easy and you will have to try hard. Change over.

74

A. If there are enough unihoc sticks, practise dribbling about the space. If not, some of you practise hand-bouncing (try to beat your own record) and some try with a padder bat. This is not easy and you will have to try hard. Change over.

Repetition of Activity C Lesson 9. The same teaching points apply to bouncing with a padder bat as to bouncing with the hands: a slow ball is recommended. Allow children to experiment with different types, see Activity A Lesson 9.

B. Organisation: Green and Yellow groups continue with Activity A.

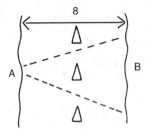

B(i) Demonstrate to Red and Blue groups Activity **B(i)** Lesson 9.

It may be appropriate to place ropes to limit the distance for this game. If the rope is brought closer to the cones the children's reactions to receiving information will have to be faster; if it is placed further away it gives more time to predict. In this way the game can be differentiated for mixed ability groups.

B(ii) Demonstrate to Green and Yellow groups Activity **B(ii)** Lesson 9.

C. Return to Activity **A** Lesson 10.

An airflight ball is suitable for this practice. Check the grip on the unihoc stick.

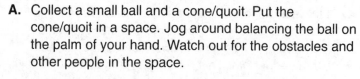
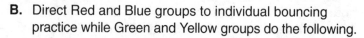

A. Collect a small ball and a cone/quoit. Put the cone/quoit in a space. Jog around balancing the ball on the palm of your hand. Watch out for the obstacles and other people in the space.

Ask the children to stretch out their arm so that they can keep their head up and are able to see the ball *and* other people.

B. Direct Red and Blue groups to individual bouncing practice while Green and Yellow groups do the following.

With a partner. Equipment: hoops/rope circles/squares, beanbag/large soft balls. Stand in the hoop, etc. Throw the beanbag/ball underarm so that your partner can catch it.

Demonstrate the above to Red and Blue groups.

Look for accurate two-handed (ball)/one-handed (beanbag) underarm throws which have a high, slow trajectory through the air. This gives more time for the receiver to make a decision. Ask the receiver to watch the ball/beanbag from the sender's hand and catch it using a downward cradle. Praise correct decisions by the receiver even if he/she does not catch the ball. Large soft balls are easier to catch than beanbags. Quickly progress to medium and small balls. Intervene in receiving skills.

The distance between the partners should not be decreased because this speeds up the flight of the ball and leaves less time for decision making.

To progress a receiving activity ask the sender to throw slightly to the left/right of the receiver. To start with, the sender can tell the receiver which way he/she is going to send the ball. This increases success and co-operation.

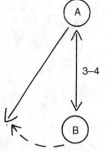

C. With a partner. One ball between two. A leads carrying the ball/beanbag. When I say 'Change', A turns and passes the ball/beanbag through the air to B. Now B leads. Continue.

A. Go and stand in a space of your own. When I say 'Walk', 'Jog', or 'Run' do so. Be careful not to bump into anyone else.

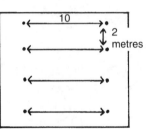

Change instructions regularly. This change of speed activity is good for warm ups because it is very active and can be used to show children the effects exercise has on their body. For example, Have you noticed that you are breathing faster? Do you feel warmer? Do you know why this happens?

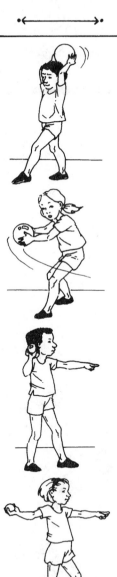

B. With a partner, ten paces apart (mark with a beanbag). One ball between two. Throw the ball across the gap through the air.

Safety: set up so that everyone throws across the same space and are a couple of metres apart. Use light balls: foam or airflight. Do not use tennis balls because they travel too far and hurt if children get hit in the face. This practice is best done outside away from walls which children might back into.

Ask children to experiment with any type of throw which gets the ball across the gap. You will see different methods, depending on the size of the ball. Overhead, slings, chest pushes for large ball; underarm and overarm throws for small balls.

Teach that the ball must start in a backswing position to generate maximum power in the throw. Ask children to find out where they must release the ball to get it across the gap ... Low down? Very high? Progress to overarm throwing using a small ball. This lesson could be repeated several times.

C. Find a space, jog on the spot. When I say 'Amber' run on the spot; when I say 'Green' stride away into a space; when I say 'Red' slow down and jog on the spot. Repeat until totally exhausted!

A. Find a space and jog on the spot. When I say 'Amber' run on the spot; when I say 'Green' stride away into a space; when I say 'Red' slow down and jog on the spot. Continue.

Repetition of Activity C Lesson 12. This activity can be used to show children the effects exercise has on their body. For example, you can ask them: Are you breathing faster? Do you feel warmer? Do you know why this happens? It can also teach them that to accelerate they need to lift their knees and move their legs and arms faster.

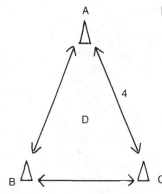

B. Organisation: Red and Blue groups practise individual bouncing, trying to beat own record or bouncing and moving slowly.

Demonstrate the Possession game to Yellow and Green groups. Groups of four: three versus one. Equipment: one medium/large ball, three beanbags/quoits.

A, B and C *roll* the ball between each other and try to keep it away from D. If D touches the ball, he/she swaps place with A, B, or C. If after six passes D has not touched the ball, swap with A, B, or C anyway.

Demonstrate the game to Red and Blue groups so that they can play.

marked person

guard

free person

The idea is for the players in possession to make the correct decision about who to pass to and for the person trying to intercept to guess which way the ball will roll – not easy! The triangle shape gives the person in possession a choice so the game will never be in 'stalemate'. Praise fast correct decisions.

This game can be played with five (four versus one) but there will be less involvement.

C. Staying in fours as a basis for partners, take one ball between two and travel around the space close to your partner passing the ball between each other. Count how many passes you can make.

A. Play Pass the braid. Some children wear coloured braids; these are the catchers. When a catcher touches another person, the catcher gives the braid to him/her and the caught person becomes a catcher.

To make the game very active at least a third of the class should have braids.

Safety: play in a defined area. Ask the children to be careful of walls, windows and the edges of playgrounds. Insist on skilful dodging, not running at full speed.

B. Organisation: Yellow and Green groups continue Activity **A**. Demonstrate the Dodging game to Red and Blue groups.

Groups of four. Equipment: enough beanbags/ropes/quoits/cones to make a square, one medium/large soft ball.

A and B roll the ball to hit C and D below the knee. C and D cannot go outside the grid. When one of dodgers is caught he/she joins the rollers. When both are caught, A and B become the dodgers. Continue.

Demonstrate the game to Green and Yellow groups.

The dodgers should act as moving targets, using good footwork and jumping to avoid the ball.

C. Find a space and jog on the spot. When I say 'Amber' run on the spot; when I say 'Green' stride away into a space; when I say 'Red' slow down and jog on the spot. Continue.

Repetition of Activity C Lesson 12.

A. Repeat Activity **A** Lesson 14.

The catchers wear a braid. The other children carry a ball of their choice. When caught they swap the ball for the catchers' braid and become 'catchers'.

B. With a partner. Play games using the following equipment:

Red group: three hoops, one large ball, four ropes.

Blue group: two padder bats, one small ball, four beanbags.

Green group: three cones, four quoits, one rope.

Yellow group: one padder bat, six beanbags, one airflight ball.

(You can provide the list of equipment on a card for each colour group.)

Each group must use all the equipment (some may have to be borrowed from other groups). Threes can play as well as partners.

Intervene in the spacing of the 'game' for safety. Ask the children to explain to you how they made their game (rule structure) and how they have changed it.

This lesson can be the basis for several others by rotating the equipment to other groups.

C. Let some groups show/explain their game to another group.

'They talk about what they and others have done, and are able to make simple judgements.'

(End of Key Stage Description, Key Stage 1 1994)

These 'pre'-invasion, net, and fielding/striking activities are designed to introduce children at the age of 7–8 to using travelling, sending and receiving skills in the context of an activity which for example:

- invades or defends a space, or retains possession;
- uses a 'net' to play through or over, changing sender and receiver roles each time the ball 'crosses' the net;
- throws/hits the ball away from fielders who try to prevent strikers scoring,

and therefore works toward the understanding of decisions about attacking and defending in these game contexts.

The activities which follow are progressions. For more detailed lesson plans see *Development of Games and Athletic Skills* (Year 3 and Year 4 material, pp. 28–77).

Invasion

Hit the cone

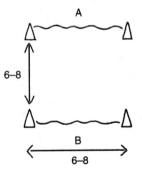

With a partner. Equipment: medium ball, ropes, four cones/quoits, etc. A rolls the ball from behind the rope to try to hit B's cones, etc. (attack). B tries to intercept before the ball hits the cone (defence) but must stand behind the rope line. B now has possession and the game proceeds.

Ask receivers where they are going to stand to receive the ball. If the receiver stops a scoring pass they should aim at the undefended cone.

Development
The targets can be moved further apart. Does this make it easier to attack or defend the cones?

Invent a game using three targets each.

Passing moving forwards
Equipment: grids, cones for markers, balls. Set up the cones in two rows.

With a partner (or in threes). One of you has the ball. Walk forwards, side by side, holding the ball in two hands; pass

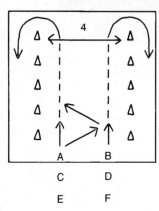

the ball to each other. When you get to the end of the markers, turn and return to the start on the outside of the markers.

Children should be close to their partners and use a medium ball, passing with a sideways swing pass (rugby type). This is an essential skill for later passing games.

Development
Ask the children to try jogging, try using feet, then unihoc stick.

Change ball

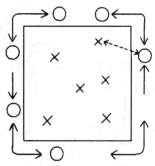

With partner. Equipment: grids, one ball between two. Players inside the grid travel about carrying the ball. Players outside the grid jog around the grid, sometimes changing direction, ready to receive the ball on the signal 'Change'. The partner carrying the ball passes to the partner outside the grid and they change over.

Passes can be rolled, bounced, or through the air. Senders must look up, spot the receiver, and ensure they are 'free' to be passed to. This teaches those 'in possession' to scan as they travel for people on their own side to pass to.

Development
Receivers can signal for the ball when they want it instead of waiting for the teacher's signal. Senders now have to look up more frequently to watch their partner.

Possession ball

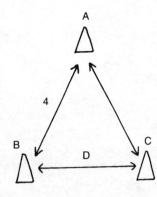

As Year 2 Lesson 13.

Development
Instead of rolling the ball to each other, the passers try to pass the ball using bounces or through the air passes.

Net Activities

Three cone game

With a partner. Equipment: three cones/quoits, etc., one medium ball, ropes. Roll the ball through the cones to make your partner move.

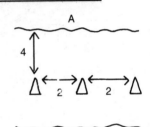

Senders have to make decisions about where to send the ball. Receivers have to make decisions about where they stand to receive it. The cones are the 'net'.

Development
Sidelines can be introduced and the cones moved further apart. Play with a small ball. Use three hoops and bounce the ball into the hoops.

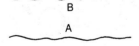

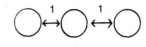

Skittle game

With a partner. Equipment: two skittles, garden cane, a medium ball, ropes (a rope with beanbags tied to the ends can also make a net). Throw the ball over the net to bounce once before it is caught by your partner.

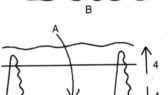

Senders have to make decisions about where to send the ball. Receivers have to make decisions about where they stand to receive it.

Development
Sidelines can be introduced. Play with a small ball. Hoops can be placed to throw into. The distance of the hoops can be varied.

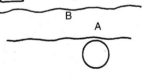

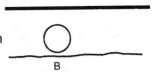

Striking/fielding activities

Sector game

With a partner. Equipment: five hoops (rope circles), medium ball. A throws the ball to B, who catches the ball and then throws the ball into one of the targets (1, 2, 3). A retrieves the ball. After three throws change roles.

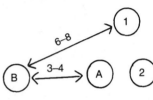

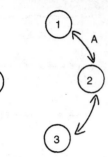

Scoring can be used. This practice teaches the sender to use all the space, without using hitting skills.

Development 1
B drops a small, foam ball and hits it with a bat towards the hoops. Vary the hoop distances from the striker. A is now released as a fielder and rolls the ball back to B.

Development 2
Play in threes, with two fielders, defending three hoops.

Throwing game
With a partner (or in threes or fours). Equipment: three hoops, three ropes, three beanbags each. Each player takes three throws from whichever rope he/she chooses. Use overarm throws. Develop throwing accuracy.

Development
Use airflow balls. Increase distances to target hoops. Hoops can also be smaller.

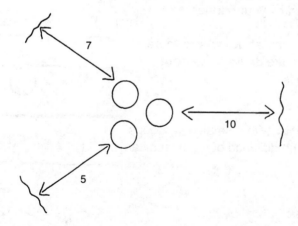

Award schemes

PEGS Awards (Physical Education Games Skills)

The Scheme is designed for children in the 5–8 age range and has four award levels involving travelling, sending and receiving skills.

Full details are available from:

Physical Education Association
Ling House, 5 Western Court
Bromley Street
Digbeth
Birmingham B9 4AN